TRACKING COUGARS

THE BASICS

James C. Halfpenny

TRACKING COUGARS

THE BASICS

James C. Halfpenny

Tracking Cougars: The Basics
Preface to the Reprinted Edition

Sometime over 63 years ago, I read a book from my local library called Animal Tracks and Hunter Signs by Ernest Thompson Seton. Seton is arguably the "godfather" of tracking, as most trackers since his time can be traced to his inspiration. I, certainly, am one of those trackers Seton "Fathered." His book hooked me on natural history, especially tracking.[1]

If you check the plaster casts in the Track Education Center Museum in Gardiner, Montana, you will find casts I made dated 1958. These are the oldest casts I still have; there may have been earlier ones though.

The casts are of raccoon tracks. Those raccoon casts carry a fond memory of Dabbles The Coon from Animal Tracks and Hunter Signs. Your assignment as a tracker is to read Dabbles' story and Seton's book. While you are at it, check out all the books by Seton!

Now I am in my 75th trip around the sun (74 on January 23, 2021) and my eighth decade of "following the trail." It is time to share the plethora of knowledge I have been fortunate enough to gain.

With the changing world, no one will ever get to live the life and walk the trails that I have. Few will ever track the seven continents, explore the tracking seasons and live nature at its prime as I have. Climate change helps guarantee my claim. I wish to share my experiences and hard gained knowledge through a series of books called Halfpenny Tracks.

Halfpenny Tracks are publications about my lifetime of natural history and tracking experiences. Tracking Cougars is but one of those books. Tracking Cougars is for all trackers who wish to study tracks from the members of the cat family: cougars, bobcat, lynx, jaguars, ocelot and jaguarundi. Tracking Cougars was the first of my species specific quick guides to tracking. It is the quick guide to verifying the presence of cougars and many aspects of the book are applicable to the other felid species. I wrote it in 1992 and it still represents an important contribution to tracking knowledge. Thus it is reprinted now.

1 Ernest Thompson Seton wrote and illustrated with his hand drawings, a myriad of natural history books from the beginning to past the middle of the 20th century including the classics such as LIves of Game Animals, Two LIttle Savages, Wild Animals I have Known, The Biography oHello Amy.f a Grizzly, and Wild Animals at Home which could be called Wild Animals of Yellowstone. Seton was also the Chief Tracker of the Boy Scouts of America.

Dedicated to Harley Shaw, consummate lion field researcher and all around outstanding individual. It was Harley that first recognized the need for a field guide to tracking mountain lions. Harley has enjoyed and endured a life-time of lion research, conservation, and management concerns. Anyone considering himself/herself worthy of being a lion researcher, tracker, or natural historian must be intimately familiar with Harley's book Soul Among Lions (The 1994 Rocky Mountain Lyceum, Resound Recordings, POB 5333, Estes Park, CO 80517).

Thank you Harley Shaw!

Acknowledgments

Many individuals have influenced my thinking about tracking and the production of this book. Some I have not met, but their work and writings have been instrumental in my thought process. I wish to acknowledge the influence, input, and help of Lee Fitzhugh, Nan Lederer, Cindy McAllister, Olaus Murie, Kerry Murphy, Diane Renkin, Michael Sanders, Ernest Thompson Seton, Harley Shaw, Dave Slovisky, Shawn Smallwood, Rick Thompson, and Ralph Waldt. To all my students and any whom I have missed - thank you. Special thanks to Diann Thompson for her encouragement.

Learning About Tracking

A Naturalist's World is dedicated to providing educational programs and materials about natural history and ecology, including tracking, animal behavior and cold region studies. ANW provides classes and products facilitating tracking. Classes are species specific (black, grizzly, or polar bears, wolves, lion, lynx, wolverine, fisher, marten, or ungulates), deal with the science of tracking (basic, advanced, snow, research, management) or emphasize a season or area (winter, alpine, Arctic).

TRACKING COUGARS

INTRODUCTION

Tracking Cougars: The Basics provides images to aid in understanding mountain lion, *Felis concolor*, signs in the field and to serve as a basic teaching collection for classroom use. It is designed to provide a photographic, introductory coverage of footprints, gaits, trails, scat, scent marking, tree clawing, kills, and burials. Emphasis is placed on obtaining standardized measurements of sign and the use of measurements to identify tracks and estimate sexes of animals. All slides of sign were taken in the field and do not represent captive situations. This book is also available as a computer program or 35mm slide show.

Tracking Cougars: The Basics is designed as the starting point for the study of mountain lion signs. The slides should aid in ecological studies where populations of lions exist. They may be used to train volunteers to run survey routes to detect and monitor the presence of lions. Tracking Cougars should also aid in detection surveys where the presence of lions is suspect or where lions are very rare. For these purposes, emphasis has been placed on separating lion tracks from those of domestic dogs. I have provided a criteria sheet for separating dog and lion tracks, and a detailed minimum outline database for the "average" adult mountain lion from Colorado, Wyoming, and Montana. If lions are rare or have been non-existent for a long period, such as in the case of the eastern panther, seek additional verification of track identification from a knowledgeable person experienced in tracking lions. It is best to record tracks permanently in the form of photographs or plaster casts (Halfpenny 1987, Halfpenny et al. 1995).

Selected readings including pictorials for those who appreciate the beauty of the cougar and all cats are provided (see bibliography). David Baron's book, The Beast in the Garden, relates the story of Dr. Halfpenny's field research and experience with human / mountain lion interactions and managment issues especially in Colorado. Contact Dr. Halfpenny for information on field seminars about tracking and verification of cougars and human / mountain lion interactions, especially around communities.

Excellent overview articles include Hansen (1992) and Tinsley (1987). Biological summary articles include Dixon (1982) , Lindzey (1987), Kitchener (1991) and Seidensticker (1991). For taxonomic and historical perspectives see Hall (1981), and Goldman (1946) and Young (1946) respectively. Shaw (1989) provides insight into the management of lions. Additional tracking references include Halfpenny (1987, 1997, 1998), Halfpenny et al. (1995) and Shaw (1983).

Please let me offer some helpful hints to the would be lion tracker. Be careful of the tracking scene. Once clues are stepped on they are usually irretrievable! Gather all the clues before you deduce what happened. Avoid jumping to conclusions! Avoid single factor reasoning, because seldom does one clue tell the entire story. Good natural history detectives use the diagnostic suite of characteristics to solve a tracking mystery. This means that the entire collection of characteristics, not a single clue, lead to the answer. Often an important clue will not be present or may be "out voted" by many less important clues.

Cougar or Mountain Lion or Puma or Panther or Painter or Catamount?

What do we call this magnificent creature known to scientists as *Felis concolor*? Over 200 names have been used for this cat since the Europeans first arrived in North America. Native American, Spanish, British, French each had their names. These names have been in use for hundreds of years. People tend to favor their regional names, but all common names are correct. Only the scientific name, *Felis concolor*, does not vary from region to region or around the world.

Cougar and mountain lion are common names I choose to use. Cougar represents a purely North American name while mountain lion recognizes the presence of this cat in the mountainous west where I do most of my work. Least we get too possessive of our favorite name, remember that in South America there are still different names for cougar, some probably around much longer than names we use.

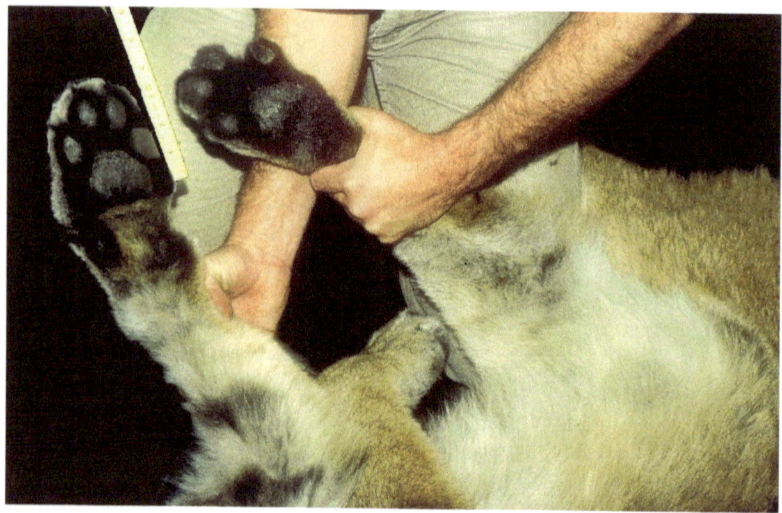

COUGAR FOOT ANATOMY

Left front and hind feet of a cougar. The feet of cougars differ substantially between front and hind and between right and left. Shown here are the left feet of a young adult male cougar. The center of gravity in carnivores, including lions, is closer to the front feet because the head extends well forward of the front feet. Therefore, front feet are larger than hind. Note that the front feet tend to be rounder, while the hind feet tend to be longer than wide and are more dog-like in this character.

Cougar front foot with ruler. The outline of the front foot is relatively round. Toes or digits are numbered from the inside (medial) of the foot outward (lateral). Toe number 1 on the front foot is a dew claw located high on the inside of the leg. The dew claw (also known as the "killer claw" because of its ripping potential) is only attached by ligaments, but still functions for grasping. The dew claw does not show in tracks and since it doesn't touch the ground, it remains very sharp.

Four toes show on the bottom of the foot and in the track. The inside toe (2) is larger than the outside toe (5). Therefore, this is a left front foot. Note the tear-drop shape of the toes with narrow anterior points. Toe 3 is positioned slightly anterior to the rest of the toes.

Claws usually do not show as they are drawn up by ligaments and hidden on the upper surface of the foot. A rough callus pad exists high on the inside of the foot and only shows in deep prints in the snow or mud.

A large pad extends forward (anterior) between the toes and is known as the interdigital pad. The interdigital pad is relatively large and in the front foot is both absolutely larger than that of the hind foot

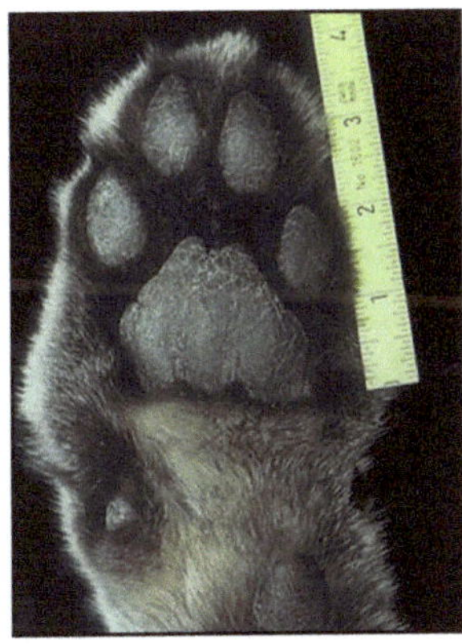

and covers relatively more space in the foot than that of the hind foot.

The leading edge (anterior) of the interdigital pad has two lobes. There are three lobes on the posterior edge of the pad. The medial lobe may be even with, shorter than, or longer than the lateral lobes. Leading edges of the pad are nearly straight and the inside edge has a distinct angle. Trackers should be able to easily identify right from left footprints using either toe size, toe position, or interdigital pad shape.

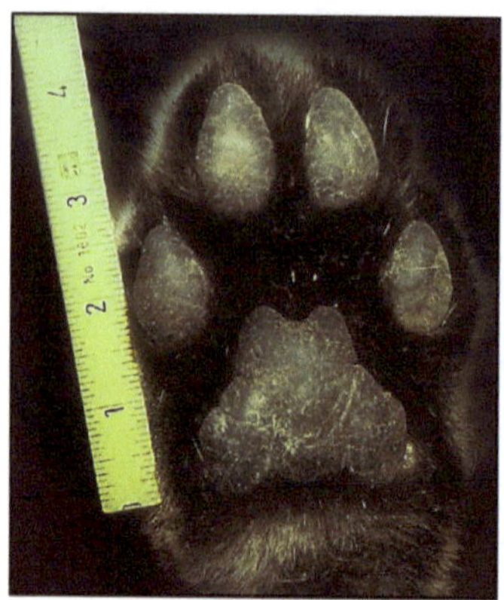

Cougar Hind Foot with Ruler. The outline of the hind foot is longer than wide. No dew claw is present on the hind foot.

Four toes show on the bottom of the foot and in the track. The inside toe (2) is larger than the outside (5). Toes are tear-drop shaped and toe 3 leads the rest of the toes.

The leading edge of the interdigital pad has two lobes which are often more clearly defined than those of the front feet. The lateral edges of the pad are concave. The pad covers relatively less space in the hind footprint.

Note: the hind and front footprints in Murie (1954) and Shaw (1979) were incorrectly labeled. Labels should be reversed, the front feet are actually hind and hind feet are actually front.

Cougar Foot Anatomy and Footprint Morphology

Cougar Hind and Front Footprints. The differences in feet are clearly seen in footprints. The front print is larger and rounder than the hind. Front toes may also splay more. The hind footprint is smaller and relatively longer than wide. The great difference in size between front and hind feet often causes observers to believe two lions have passed. The knife is 5 1/8 inches long.

Cougar left front footprint with ruler. Note the asymmetrical position of the toes, leading third toe, presence of tear-drop shaped toes, bilobate anterior margin of the interdigital pad.

TRACKING COUGARS

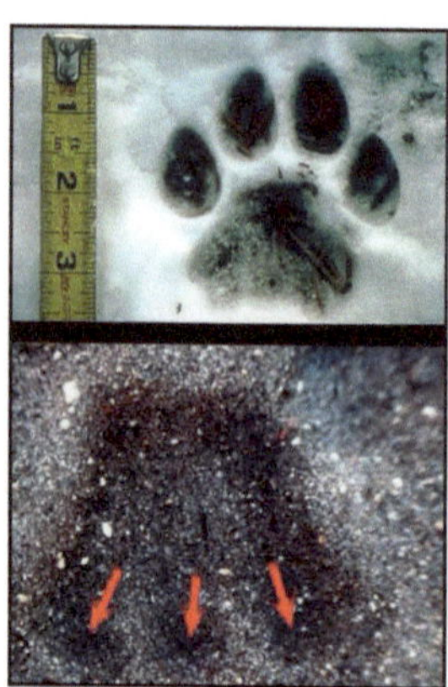

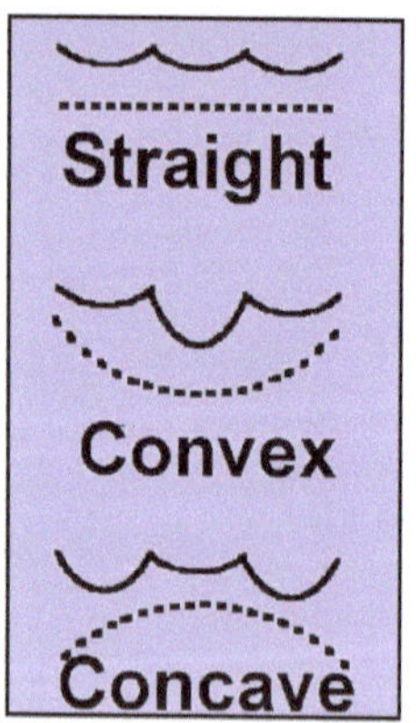

Cougar left front track with details.
When the anterior lobes of the interdigital pad are indistinct in the footprint, the anterior edge will be relatively flat and broad. The anterior end of the pad usually appears deeper than the posterior end. Some trackers visualize the deeper impression of the anterior end of the pad as raised half-moon-shaped ridge of substrate in front of the interdigital pad. Medial lobes of the pad are impressed as deep as the lateral lobes.

Some authors in the past have suggested using the posterior edges of the interdigital pad as a main clue for separating cougar tracks from canids (wolves and dogs). A line is drawn touching the posterior edges of the lateral lobes. The idea is that in cougar tracks the medial lobe will touch the line, a condition called straight. In canid tracks, the medial lobe will be anterior to the line, called concave.

Smallwood and Fitzhugh (1989) have quantified this relationship for cougars and dogs (see table next page) and have shown that in about 66% of the cases, the lion track will show the straight configuration; the rest of the time it will be either concave or convex. In about 48% of the cases, dogs tracks show the straight configuration. while the presence of the straight condition is a clue that the footprint is that of a lion, it should be interpreted in the context of all clues and is NOT the definitive clue.

Shape of the posterior edge of the interdigital pad of cougars and dogs. Numbers shown are the approximate percentage of a species tracks which fall into each category (after Smallwood and Fitzhugh, 1989).

Species	Concave	Shape Straight	Convex
Cougar	14%	66%	20%
Dog	46%	48%	6%

The arc of toes differs between cats and canids. A marginal line drawn touching the anterior edges of the toes is relatively rounded in cats or "stair-stepped" in dogs.

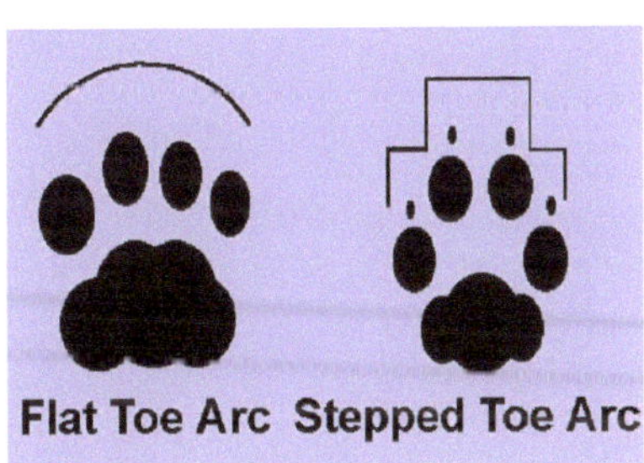

TRACKING COUGARS

Domestic Dog Tracks. Top photograph shows a good example of a domestic dog footprint. Front footprint (larger) is shown on the left, in back of the hind print. Prominent broad claws are present. The arc of toes is "stair-stepped", and a marginal line drawn touching the front of the leading edge of the toes forms distinct steps. The leading edge of the interdigital pad has a single, pointed lobe. The interdigital pad of dogs is relatively small compared to that of a lion. The interdigital pad of the lion occupies most of the footprint, where as in dogs it occupies a smaller proportion.

Bottom photograph shows a dog footprint that observers mistook for a cougar track. Part of the confusion about this track is the fact that it lacked claws. The lack of claws is a tendency found in prints of larger dogs! Dogs, just like humans, have nails or claws originating on the top of their digits. The larger the dog, the more rounded the pad on the bottom of the digit. Therefore, the greater the likelihood that the claw will be held high enough off the ground that it may not show in the majority of the footprints.

Note that toes are nearly equal in size and position. Individual toes lack the tear-drop shape of a cougar. Lateral toes are set back so that a line drawn touching the front of the leading edge of the toes is stair-stepped. The print appears longer than wide.

The posterior portion of the interdigital pad registers deeper and more prominently in the ground than the anterior portion, the reverse situation of lion tracks. Although very faint, it appears that the anterior edge of the interdigital pad has but one lobe. Lateral lobes (wings) are faint; in lions they are prominent.

Criteria for evaluating suspected cat tracks. The summary sheet below provides a mechanism for checking off different clues in a suspected footprint as part of the investigation process.

Criteria for Evaluating Felid Tracks

Felids in General
print: - round, wider than long (especially the front footprint)
claws: - lacking
toes:
    number   - four (polydactyl exceptions)
    size   - graduated, large toe on the medial side of the foot
    arc   - flattened, rounded leading margin
    position   - asymmetrical
Interdigital pad
    size   - relatively large
    anterior   - bilobate, anterior end prominent
    medial lobes   - lobes are level with center of pad
    gait   - walking, jumping
    behavior   - cat-like

Bobcats
print size: relatively small
pad marks: clear -- lacking hair around pads (hair increases in winter)
depression: sinking deeply into the snow for track's size
interdigital pad: anterior bilobate, posterior strongly develop and trilobate
tail drag: lacking

Lynx
print size: relatively large
pad marks: indistinct - haired foot
depression: sinking shallowly into the snow for its size
toe registration: weak, toes may show on hard or spring snow
interdigital pad: obscured by hair; appearing indistinct & large or small & prominent
tail drag: lacking

Lion
print size: relatively large
pad marks: clear - lacking hair around pads (hair increases in winter)
depression: sinking deeply into the snow for track's size
interdigital pad: anterior bilobate, posterior strongly developed and trilobate
tail drag: may be present

TRACKING COUGARS

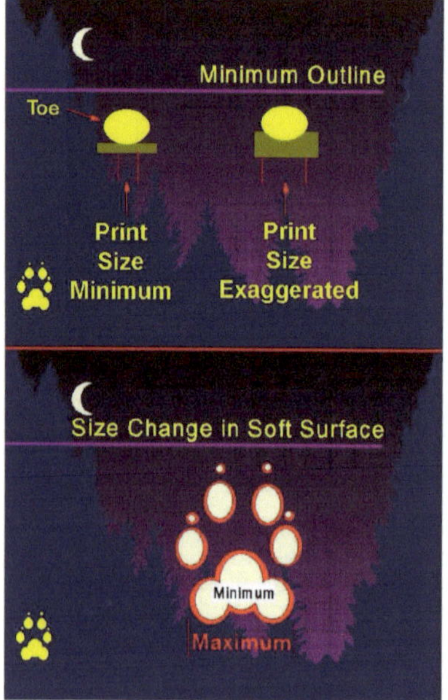

Minimum Outline Method. Increasing human populations have caused more interactions with mountain lions necessitating greater accuracy in understanding lion tracks. To standardize and improve accuracy, footprints are measured using the minimum outline method.

The deeper feet sink into a substrate, be it soil or snow, the larger footprints appear and one animal may create what appears to be many different sized footprints in varying substrates. It is necessary to standardize the measurement of tracks so that a series of tracks in different substrates yields only one consistent set of measurements. To standardize measurements, we use a method now called the minimum outline method (from research by Smallwood and Fitzhugh 1993).

Place your hand on a hard surface. Feel the outline of your handprint on that surface. That is the minimum outline of your hand. If your hand were sinking into the mud, the outline would increase in size. We call the larger series of outlines when the hand sinks deeper, the variable (or maximum) outline because their sizes would depend on how deep your hand sinks into the surface. Your hand could leave an infinite number of different sized prints.

Minimum outline measurements for footprints of adult cougars (mm).

Foot	Length	Width	Interdigital Pad Length	Interdigital Pad Width
Front	81.6	91.7	35.7	50.0
Hind	84.3	91.4	37.4	48.1

In cross-section, the picture illustrates the outline left by one finger on a hard surface (top left) and on a soft surface (top right). The finger sinking deeper into the surface will create an exaggerated print size. To measure the minimum outline, try to judge the break point where the edges of the pads would turn away from the hard surface. Measure only to that point. The rounded upper edges of the pad falsely increase footprint size and are not measured.

It is important to use the conservative, but more consistent measurement of minimum outline to avoid false impressions of larger animals. Track impressions in the mind are based on area (bottom). The variable outline increases, not as the simple linear addition to footprint size, but with the mathematical square of the linear measurements. In short, a few extra millimeters of width and length give the false impression of a much larger footprint. The importance of this effect cannot be over emphasized. While there is some subjectivity in judging the break point, we have found through many tests that people trained to use minimum outline measurements for carnivore tracks will dramatically reduce the variation in measurements of tracks from individual animals and among observers.

The above table lists a set of minimum outline for adult cougars from the Rocky Mountain Region.

TRacKinG couGars

Width measurements of interdigital pads for tracks made by male and female lions.

Footprint	Sex:	Male	Female
Front		57-75 mm	49-58 mm
Hind		49-64 mm	41-60 mm

Measurements compiled for Colorado (Anderson 1992), Yellowstone (Murphy 1993), California and Arizona (Shaw 1979). Measurements are of variable outlines.

Although considerable difference in body size occurs between subspecies of cougars, measurements of the interdigital pad width may be used to separate sexes of adult cougars (table above). Cougars with the width of the front print interdigital pads equal to or wider than 59 mm or hind print interdigital pads equal to or wider than 61 mm are males; smaller male tracks do occur.

Potential Combinations of footprints (interdigital pad width in mm)

Lion Tracks Observed	Interpretation
Single Set of Tracks	
Pad >=59	Adult male
Pad 50 - 58	Adult female or transient subadult male or female
Two Sets of Tracks	
Pad >=59 & Pad 50 - 58	Breeding pair which may remain together for up to 10 days
both sets with pads 50 - 58	Adult female with yearling or newly independent litter mates traveling together
one with pad 50 - 58; other smaller than 50	Adult female with single young, recently independent litter mates still traveling together
Three or More Sets	Female with litter. Pads less than 40 mm are dependent kittens and tracks of mature female should be nearby

Using interdigital pad measurements, Shaw (1979) suggested interpretations of various track combinations (table above). These combinations help identify cougars in a given area and provide a picture of the population structure.

Note: cutoff sizes may vary for different subspecies. The criteria listed here use a higher cutoff (50 mm) for adult female lions than the 40 mm criteria used by Shaw (1979). This is based on more recent information from Colorado (Anderson 1992) and Yellowstone (Murphy 1993).

TRACKING COUGARS

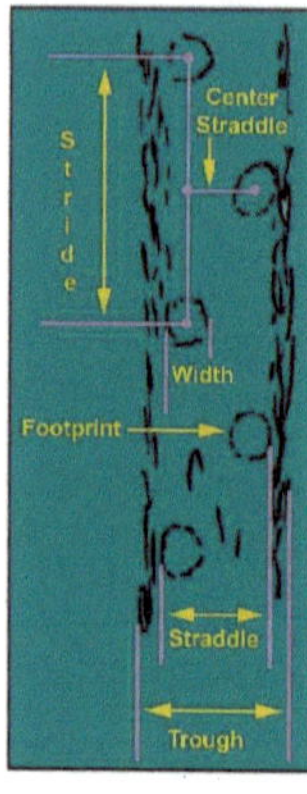

Trail Measurements. Often it is not possible to discern sufficient detail in footprints to distinguish cougar tracks from other carnivores or sometimes even from ungulates. In these cases, trackers may gather clues from the trail left by the animal. We use four different measurements to provide additional clues for identification: stride, straddle, center straddle, and trough (Halfpenny, et al. 1996).

Stride is the distance from where a point on a foot hits the surface to where the same point on the same foot touches the surface again (Muybridge 1957). A stride is one complete cycle of locomotion. A stride of a quadruped using all four feet for locomotion consists of four footprints. Measuring stride in this manner provides a relative estimate of speed as gaits change. A group is a subunit of a stride consisting of all four footprints, two fronts, two hinds, and conversely two rights, and two lefts.

Straddle is the distance from the left outside edge of a print in a group to the right outside edge of a print in the same group. Use outside straddle measurement because inside straddle of carnivores often overlaps.

The edge of tracks in snow is often difficult to discern because of melting or blowing snow. However, the human eye is very good at determining the center of a track. Therefore, we use center measurements for clues to animal identification. Place a survey flag or mark the center of each footprint in the section of trail to be measured. Center stride can be measured directly from these marks. Center straddle is measured by drawing a line between the center marks of two consecutive footprints on the same side of the trail. The center straddle is then measured from the center of the footprint on the other side of the trail to the perpendicular point on the center line.

Trough is the distance from the left outside

Trail Measurements and Estimating Cougar Weights

Estimating weight of cougars from stride and footprints

Weight (lbs) = 254.34 + 3.86 (walking stride [mm])
Weight (lbs) = 173.20 + 69.19 (front interdigital pad length [mm])
Weight (lbs) = 106.90 + 58.31 (hind interdigital pad length [mm])

---

edge of any hair drag mark to the right outside edge of any hair drag mark. Trough differs from straddle in that straddle is measured from the edges of the load bearing portion of the footprint, and trough is measured to include hair drag marks which occur outside the load bearing area of the footprint. The trough measurements represents the "hairiness" of the foot. Trough is particularly helpful for distinguishing lion tracks from lynx (Halfpenny et al., 1996).

Two important points - first, all trail measurements are made either parallel to the line of travel (stride) or perpendicular to the line of travel (straddle, center straddle, and trough).

Measurements should not be skewed by deviating from parallel to or right angles to the line of travel. Second, straddle refers to the distance across a trail and width refers to the distance across a single footprint.

Lion weights may be estimated from walking stride and footprint measurements. Using data provided by Kerry Murphy for cougars from the Greater Yellowstone Ecosystem, I calculated three equations for estimating weight in pounds (table above).

These equations explain 74, 95, and 89% of the variation in the data, respectively, and provide a reasonable estimate of lion weight.

TRACKING COUGARS

Detail in foot placement and tail drag. Cougars leave other signs when traveling that may provide clues for identification. Tail drag marks occasionally occur along the trail. However, for an animal with such a long tail, drag marks can be rare occurrences. Elongate metatarsal bones on the cougar's hind leg may show under different circumstances, (left hind foot in below shows the bend between the tarsal and metatarsal bones; the ankle and knee are higher on the leg). When the metatarsal touches the ground, it produces an elongate heel in the track. This heel is often seen where lions have sat waiting for prey or

crouched prior to making a final attack. The typical gait of a cougar is the walk. When walking, hind feet register directly on top of front footprints and only the hind prints may be visible. As lions start to amble, the hind print moves forward of the front print. Stride of a walking lion is about 36 to 40 inches (100 to 110 cm). When the stride extends to 50 or more inches (125 cm), the lion is trotting. Cougar trails appear straight while canids often travel with their body at an angle to the direction of travel leaving front footprints on one side of the line of travel and hind footprints on the other side.

Signs left by cougars. Signs include scat, scat burials, scrapes, and clawed trees. I am of the opinion that, at least for adult males, these signs convey information allowing competing cats to avoid each other. Signs aid in the verification of the presence of cougars.

Cougar scats vary in size, shape, and content (Halfpenny 1987). Typical adult lion scat is about 1 inch (2.5 cm) in diameter and shows segment divisions about 1 to 1.5 times as long as the scat is wide. Segments may be lacking if the lion was feeding on fresh, moist

protein. Then the scat is extruded as a single, dense paste-like cord in which segments may not be visible. Cougars break and eat bones, especially ribs but also larger bones, when feeding on a kill. Consequently their scat often contains large numbers of bone fragments. When most of the meat is gone off of a carcass, cougars will consume a considerable amount of hair which is in turn defecated. Cougars can and will scavenge old carcasses, even weeks old. In these cases, scat often contain large amounts of hair. Around fresh kill sites, several scats may be found.

TRACKING COUGARS

Mountain lions often bury their scats. The typical burial site (dung heap) is up to a yard (m) in diameter and contains a pile of scat in the center. Following defecation, the lion buries the scat by reaching over it and dragging litter on to the scat to cover it. The lion will work around the scat in a circular pattern until the scat is mostly to completely covered.

Not all lions cover their scat. In general, big males or cats trying to claim a kill may not cover scat. On the other hand, females, especially with kittens, usually bury their scat to

hide their presence from the males. Males have been known to kill kittens. When traveling longer distances, such as when dispersing, lions also may not bury their scats.

Shaw (1979) reports that female lions make mounds 4 or 5 feet (1.5 m) in diameter. These mounds may be related to birth or the presence of young. Shaw had observed only two mounds in his career. I have never observed them.

Scrape in pine duff at a burial site. In addition to scat burials, cougars will often make scrapes. A scrape looks like a burial and is made the same way. However, scrapes do not include scat. The scrape is about 12 inches (30 cm) in diameter. Lions urinate on scrapes and use them as scent markers. Each pile of litter needs to be checked to determine if it is a scent marker or scat burial. In this slide, Kerry Murphy, lion researcher, investigates a scrape near a kill site. Cougars also spray urine on to scrapes and trees, by backing up to the object and urinating a fine spray backward.

TRACKING COUGARS

Cougar clawed trees. Cougars often claw trees, perhaps to sharpen claws and perhaps to communicate information to other lions. Claw marks of a cougar standing on the ground can reach 6 feet (2 m) as Cindy McAllister shows (left photograph).

Differentiating lion trees from those of bears, marten, fisher, or wolverine is done by counting claw marks. If five claws show in footprints on the bark, then the marks were probably made by ursids or mustelids. Check closely because the little toe often does not show in every marking made by five-toed mammals.

Cougars do have a fifth claw (called the killer claw, it is attached by tendons and functions in grasping but it has no toe pad) on the front foot and it can wrap around a small diameter tree or object and once in a rare while a cougar may show five claw marks.

Claws of lions are "needle sharp" compared to claws of bears and mustelids. The sharp points of cougar claws often scrape across the bark before digging in and occasionally after exiting (right photograph).

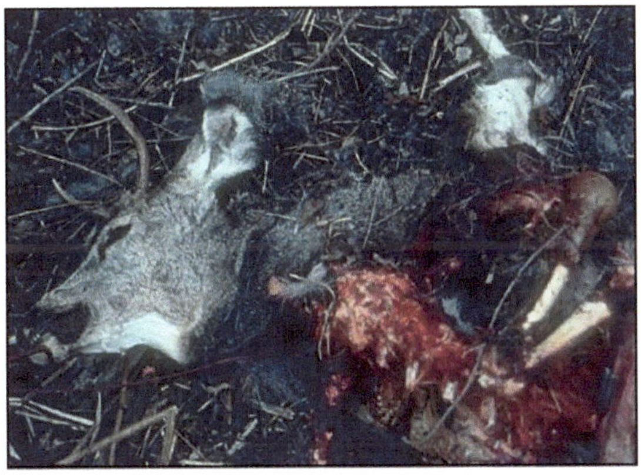

Deer killed by a cougar.
Mountain lion kill smaller prey by swatting them with a paw or biting from the top, typically at the base of the head of the prey species. Lion often kill larger prey by biting the throat from the bottom and suffocating the animal.

Occasionally cougars will jump on larger mammals, deer and elk, from the top and break their necks by grabbing the jaw on the opposite side and torquing the head around although this behavior is rare. Lions seldom take prey larger than 300-400 pounds (150-200 kg) and usually take calves of domestic cattle and elk. Rarely they will take adult bull elk .

At suspected kill sites, peeling back the skin may reveal canine tooth holes in the throat or massive hemorrhaging at the base of the skull on the back of the neck. Tooth marks from the top canine teeth are 1.5 to 2 inches (4-5 cm) apart, while those from the lower canine teeth are 1 to 1.5 inches (3-4 cm) apart. Scratch marks on the jaw or neck may indicate torquing the head around; check for broken or compressed vertebrae. Blood stains on the ground suggests that the prey was killed and not scavenged.

TRACKING COUGARS

Trail of cougar dragging a deer. Cougars tend to be secretive animals that like to dine in private. They will often carry or drag carcasses considerable distances to feed. This drag mark, photographed by Mike Sanders, shows where a cougar drug a mule deer carcass over 500 yards (500 m) to an old abandoned mine shaft to feed in seclusion.

I tracked one mountain lion that picked up a 100 lb (45 kg) mule deer by the belly with all four feet pointing in the air. In this manner, it jumped a six-foot (2 m), barbed-wire fence in four inches of snow without leaving a single sign it was carrying a deer from the earlier kill site to a burial site.

Feeding site hidden in aspen grove. Secluded feeding sites are often hidden deep in the brush, under overhangs, in deep ravines, in caves, or in mine shafts. Lion will surplus kill and I am aware of a lion killing 54 domestic sheep in one evening. Usually only one or two will be eaten. When mothers with kittens are involved, two or three kill sites of deer may be found in a small area.

Usually cougars first open the abdominal cavity and take liver, lungs, and heart. Next, they eat the fleshiest meat including large leg muscles, rump, and shoulders. Rear legs are often eaten from the underside, not the outside. Cats seldom eat stomach and intestines.

Lions chew the bones, especially ribs and vertebrae spines, more than other predators. Coyotes will also chew the smaller bones but usually after most of the meat is gone, while lions chew bones from when they first begin to consume a carcass.

TRACKING COUGARS

Deer buried by cougars. Mountain lions often bury the remnants of their food after feeding on it. They will return, often for several days, to feed until the carcass is consumed. The stomach and intestines are usually buried at the site of the first feeding.

A typical pattern would include uncovering the carcass, feeding, moving the carcass to a new location, and reburial of the carcass. Carcasses are usually moved from 10 to 25 yards (10-25 m) and a search radius of 100 yards (100 m) should yield most buried food caches. In situations of surplus killing, lions usually do not bury most carcasses.

Carcasses are buried using any available material (top photograph) including snow, grass, litter, or dirt. Lions reach across the carcass and drag the material over the carcass to achieve the best possible burial. However, often large mammals such as deer will not be completely buried, simple because there is not enough material near by to accomplish the task. In this case, legs are still showing.

A dried hide was excavated from this burial site (bottom photograph). Bones and hide are often scraped clean of all meat and other tissues. The rough tongue, a characteristic of cats, provides an excellent scraper to remove all edible material.

Track of an exceptionally large female mountain lion in Canyonlands National Park in October.

The classic lion characteristics are evident including no claws, foot wider than long, broad anterior edge on the interdigital pad, rounded leading margin. Knife is 5 1/8 inches (8.0 cm) long. The track appears larger than normal because of the soft sand which slides down into the print making it appear larger.

TRACKING COUGARS

Trail of two mountain lions. This picture shows the trail associated with the picture on page 29. Here a mother cougar and her yearling have walked down the sand bottom of a draw. Note that the tracks of the yearling appear less distinct because of its lighter weight.

Anderson, A.E., D.C. Bowden, D.M. Kattner. 1992. **The Puma on Umcompahgre Plateau, Colorado.** Tech. Rep. 40, Colorado Division of Wildlife, Fort Collins, CO.

Baron, D. 2004. **The Beast in the Garden.** W.W. Norton & Company, New York, NY.

Belden, R.C. 1978. **How to recognize panther tracks.** Proc. Ann. Conf. S.E. Assoc. Fish and Wildl. Agencies 32:112-115.

Brakefield, T. 1993. **Kingdom of Might: The World's Big Cats.** Voyageur Press, Stillwater, MN.

Currier, M.J.P. 1983. *Felis concolor.* Mammalian Species 200:1-7.

Dixon, K. 1982. **Mountain Lion.** Pp. 711-727 in Chapman, J.A. and G.A. Feldhamer (eds.). Wild Mammals of North America: Biology, Management, and Economics. Johns Hopkins University Press, Baltimore, MD.

Downing, R.L. 1979. **Differences between tracks of dogs and cougars.** Eastern Cougar Newsletter. 2 pp.

Downing , R.L. and V.L. Fifield. 1986. **Differences between tracks of dogs and cougars.** Worcester Science Center. Worcester, Mass. 2 pp.

Fitzhugh, E.L. and W.P. Gorenzel. 1985. **Design and analysis of mountain lion track surveys.** Pp. 78-87 in V.C. Bleich, (ed.) Cal-Nev. Wildlife Trans., Western Section, The Wildlife Society.

Goldman, E.A. 1946. **Classification of the races of the puma. Part 2 in The Puma: Mysterious American Cat.** American Wildlife Institute, Washington, D.C.

Halfpenny, J.C. 1987. **A Field Guide to Mammal Tracking in North America.** Second Edition. Johnson Books, Boulder, CO. 176 pp.

TRACKING COUGARS

Halfpenny, J.C. 1997. **Tracking: Mastering the Basic.** Video. A Naturalist's World, Gardiner, MT.

Halfpenny, J.C. 1998. **Scats and Tracks of the Rocky Mountains.** Falcon Publishing, Helena, MT. 144 pp.

Halfpenny, J.C., R.C. Thompson, S.C. Morse, T. Holden, and P. Rezendes. 1995. **Snow Tracking.** Pp. 91-160 in Zielinski, W.J. and T.E. Kucera (eds.). American Marten, Fisher, Lynx, and Wolverine: Survey Methods for their Detection. USDA Forest Service, General Tech. Rep. PSW-GTR-157.

Hall, E.R. 1981. **The Mammals of North America.** Volume II. John Wiley and Sons, New York.

Hansen, K. 1992. **Cougar: The American Lion.** Northland Publishing Company, P.O. Box 1389, Flagstaff, AZ 86002.

Kitchener, A. 1991. **The Natural History of the Wild Cats.** Comstock Publishing Associates, Cornell University Press, Ithaca, NY.

Kutilek, M.J., R.A. Hopkins, W.E. Clinite, and T.E. Smith. 1983. **Monitoring population trends of large carnivores using track transects.** Pages 104-106 in J.F. Bell and T. Atterbury, (eds.) Renewable resource inventories for monitoring changes and trends. College of Forestry, Oregon State Univ., Corvallis,

Lindzey, F. 1987. **Mountain Lion.** Pp. 656-669 in Novak, M., J.A. Baker, M,E. Obbard, and B. Malloch (eds.). Wild Furbearer Management and Conservation in North America. Ontario Trappers Association and Ontario Ministry of Natural Resources, Ontario, Canada.

Miller, S.D. and D.D. Everett. 1986. **Cats of the World: Biology, Conservation, and Management.** Proceedings of the Second International Symposium, 1982. Caesar Kleberg Wildlife Research Institute, College of Agriculture, Texas A&I University, Kingsville, TX 78363.

Murie, O. 1954. **Animal Tracks**. The Peterson Field guide Series. Houghton Mifflin Company, Boston.

Muybridge, E. 1957. **Animals in Motion**. Dover Publications, Inc. NY.

Panwar, H.S. 1979. **A note on tiger census technique**. Tigerpaper 6(2-3):16-18.

Savage, C. 1993. **Wild Cats: Lynx, Bobcats, Mountain Lions**. Sierra Club Books, San Francisco.

Seidensticker, J. and S. Lumpkin. 1991. **Great Cats: Majestic Creatures of the Wild**. Rodale Press, Emmaus, Penn.

Shaw, H. 1989. **Soul Among Lions**. The Cougar as Peaceful Adversary. Johnson Books, Boulder, CO.

Shaw, H.G. 1983. **Mountain lion field guide**. Ariz. Game and Fish Dept. Spec. Rep. No. 9. Phoenix. 37 pp.

Shaw, H.G., N.G. Woolsey, J.R. Wegge, and R.L. Day, Jr. 1988. **Factors affecting mountain lion densities and cattle predation in Arizona, a final report**. Ariz. Game and Fish Dept. 16 pp.

Sleeper, B. 1995. Wild Cats of the World. Crown Publishers, Inc., NY, NY.

Smallwood, K.S., and E.L. Fitzhugh. 1989. **Differentiating mountain lion and dog tracks**. Smith, R.H. (ed.). Proceedings of the Third Mountain Lion Workshop, Dec. 6-8, 1988, Prescott, AZ. Arizona Game and Fish Department.

Tinsley, J.B. 1987. **The Puma: Legendary Lion of the Americas**. Texas western Press, University of Texas at El Paso.

TRACKING COUGARS

Turbank, G. 1986. **America's Great Cats**. Northland Press, Flagstaff, AZ.

Wrigley, R.E. and R.W. Nero. 1982. **Manitoba's Big Cat: The Story of the Cougar in Manitoba**. Manitoba Museum of Man and Nature, Winnipeg, Canada.

Young, S.P. 1946. **History, Life Habits, Economic Status, and Control**. Part 1 in The **Puma: Mysterious American Cat**. American Wildlife Institute, Washington, D.C.

James C. Halfpenny

Dr. Halfpenny owns A Naturalist's World, a company dedicated to providing educational programs, books, slide shows, and videos about ecologically important subjects. Topics include rare mammalian species, tracking, winter and alpine ecology, and special ecosystems: Arctic, mountain, and African. Since 1961, Jim has taught outdoor education and environmental programs for state, federal, and private organizations including among others Aspen Center for Environmental Sciences, Audubon, Colorado Outward Bound School, Defenders of Wildlife, National Outdoor Leadership School, National Wildlife Federation, Nature Conservancy, Sierra Club, Smithsonian, Teton Science School, Wilderness Society, Yellowstone Association Institute, and various Universities.

Jim was a research associate of the Institute of Arctic and Alpine Research (INSTAAR), University of Colorado and is past Field Director of the Mountain Research Station (alpine branch of INSTAAR). Jim is also a Fellow of the Explorer's Club and veteran of all continents. He has led expeditions and programs in Antarctica, China, Ecuador, Japan, Greenland, Kenya, Tanzania, and the United States.

Jim is author of <u>Yellowstone Bears in the Wild</u>, <u>Yellowstone Wolves in the Wild</u>, <u>Discovering Yellowstone Wolves</u>, <u>A Field Guide to Mammal Tracking in North America</u>,

<u>Winter: An Ecological Handbook</u>, the regional series <u>Scats and Tracks</u>, and numerous other scientific, and popular books and articles.

Jim is listed in Who's Who in the West, Science, and the World and a Vietnam veteran. He resides in the Greater Yellowstone Ecosystem where he spends as much time in the field tracking and observing bears, wolves, lynx, cougars, and wolverine as is possible. Of course, Jim believes it is better to pursue these animals on crosscountry skis.